T0395557

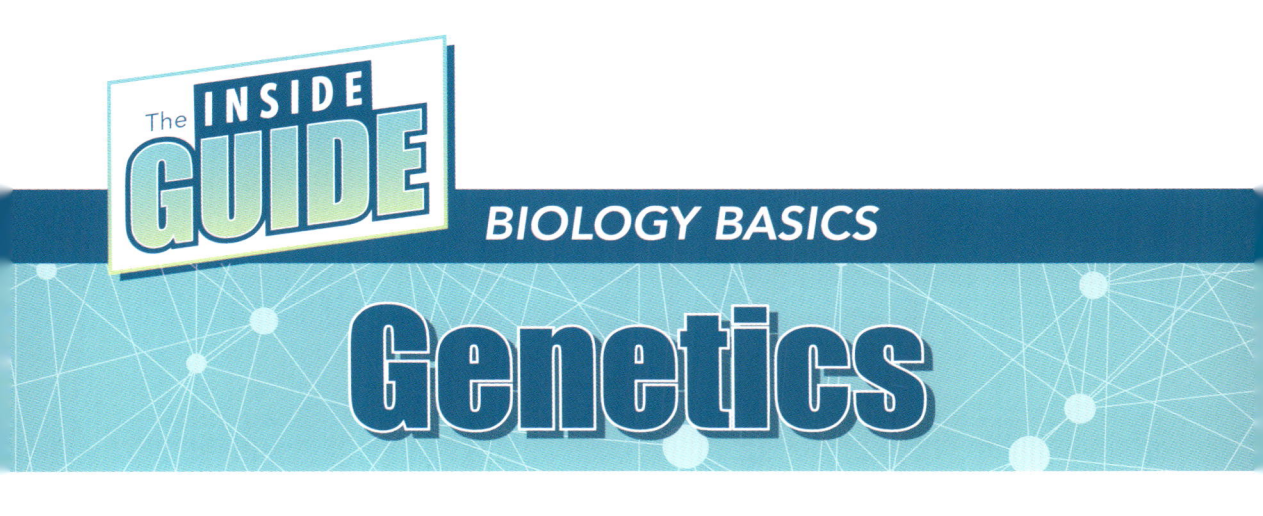

The Inside GUIDE

BIOLOGY BASICS

Genetics

By Leigh McClure

Cavendish Square

Published in 2025 by Cavendish Square Publishing, LLC
2544 Clinton Street Buffalo, NY 14224

Cataloging-in-Publication Data

Names: McClure, Leigh.
Title: Genetics / Leigh McClure.
Description: Buffalo, NY : Cavendish Square Publishing, 2025. | Series: The inside guide: biology basics | Includes glossary and index.
Identifiers: ISBN 9781502673329 (pbk.) | ISBN 9781502673336 (library bound) | ISBN 9781502673343 (ebook)
Subjects: LCSH: Genetics–Juvenile literature.
Classification: LCC QH437.5 M28 2025 | DDC 572.8–dc23

Editor: Caitie McAneney
Copyeditor: Nicole Horning
Designer: Deanna Lepovich

Find us on

CONTENTS

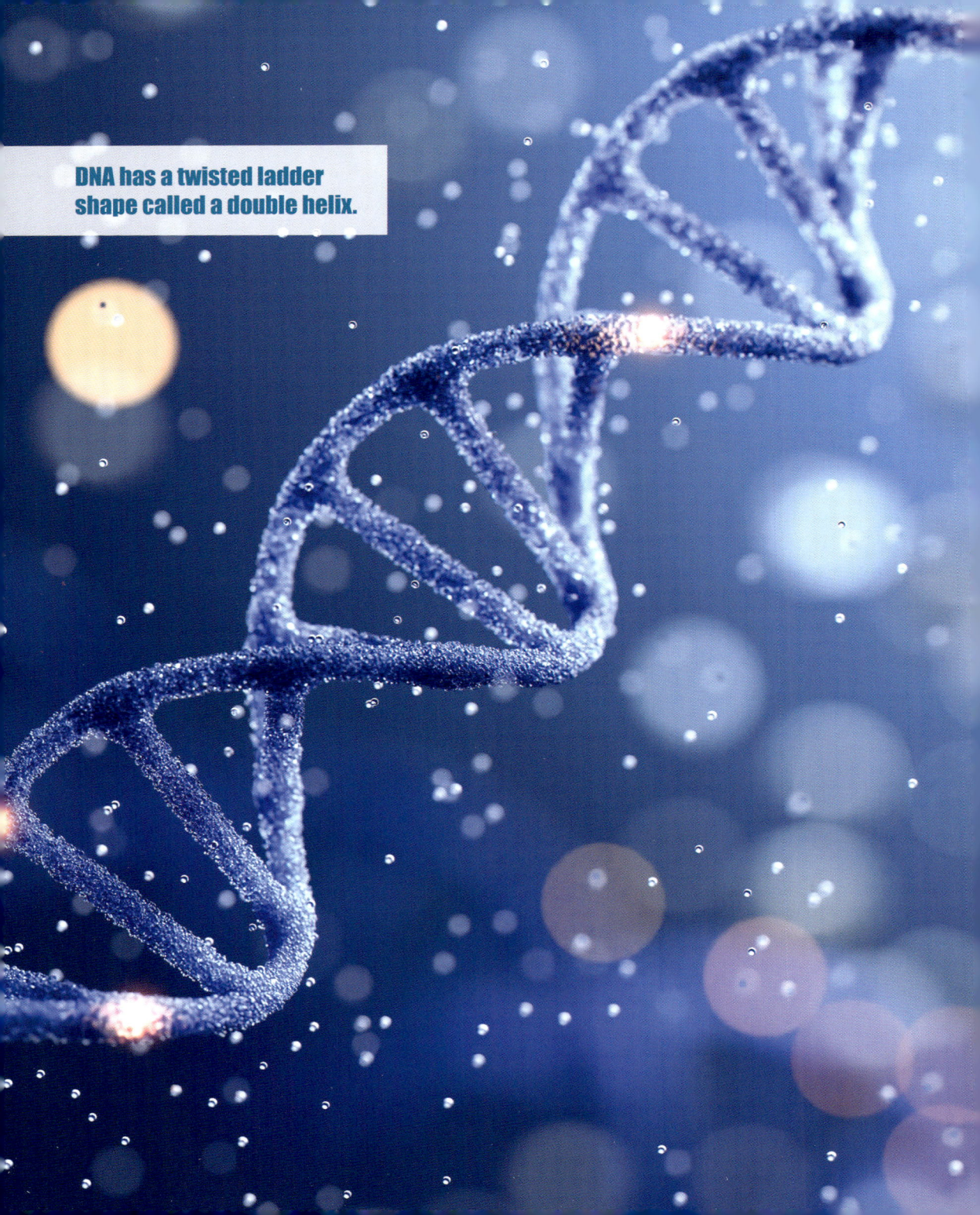

DNA has a twisted ladder shape called a double helix.

Chapter One

THE STUDY OF WHO YOU ARE

Take a moment to think about who you are. What do you look like? What are your strengths? Do you resemble your parents or siblings? Some people have the same color hair as their mother or the same eye shape as their father. Some siblings share a similar height or talents.

What makes you like your family? The study of genetics holds the answer. Genetics looks at heredity, or how features pass from parents to offspring. While you don't look exactly like either of your parents, they gave you the genes that make you who you are.

The History of Genetics

Before the 1800s, not much was known about the science behind heredity. Then, in the 1850s, Gregor Mendel began his research on plant heredity. Mendel was a **monk** from Austria, growing pea plants in his garden. He started **breeding** plants to note how traits from parent plants passed down to their offspring. Each new **generation** had traits from

Fast Fact

Pea plant heredity was easier to study than that of bees, which Gregor Mendel also attempted. However, his principles proved to be correct for plants and animals.

Mendel's Pea Plant Experiment

GENETIC TRAITS OF THE PEA PLANT (SHAPE)

P Generation (Parents)

DOMINANT TRAIT
Tall Plant
TT

× Cross-Pollination

RECESSIVE TRAIT
Dwarf Plant
tt

F1 Generation (Hybrids)

Tall Plant
Tt

Tall Plant
Tt

× Self-Pollination

Tall Plant
Tt

Tall Plant
Tt

F2 Generation

Tall Plant
TT

Tall Plant
Tt

Tall Plant
Tt

Dwarf Plant
tt

Genotyp Ratio - TT : Tt : tt
1 : 2 : 1

Phenotyp Ratio - Tall : Dwarf
3 : 1

PUNNETT SQUARE

F1 Generation (Hybrids)

	t	t
T	Tt	Tt
T	Tt	Tt

F2 Generation

	T	t
T	TT	Tt
t	Tt	tt

Mendel's experiments on the principles of heredity inspired a chart called the Punnett square, which shows the combinations of genes that may be passed from parents to offspring.

the generation before it, and the way traits were passed down seemed to follow certain principles, or rules.

Around 100 years later, the structure of DNA, or deoxyribonucleic acid, was

People were against Mendel's work when he was alive. However, by 1900, his theories were accepted and the study of genetics took off.

DARWIN AND EVOLUTION

British scientist Charles Darwin was also hard at work trying to understand the traits of living things in the mid-1800s. In the 1830s, he went to the Galápagos Islands in the Pacific Ocean. There, he studied birds called finches and noticed that finches in different areas had adapted their beak shape based on their food sources. Some had shorter, wider beaks for cracking seeds, while others had long, pointed beaks for snapping up insects. He came up with a theory that these birds had evolved—or changed over the course of generations—from a common **ancestor**. Helpful traits had been passed down until the finches in different areas had different beaks for eating.

Today, Darwin is called the "father of evolution."

Fast Fact

In 1859, Darwin published his work *On the Origin of Species*. It laid the framework for the study of evolutionary biology, or the science of life and how it changes over time.

discovered by a group of scientists. This discovery allowed scientists to take a closer look at genes, or the basic units of heredity.

Where Are Genes Found?

Every organism, or living thing, is made up of cells. Your body has special cells to carry out functions, or jobs. These functions include delivering oxygen to organs and sending messages from the brain to the rest of the body. Each cell has a nucleus, which is like the brain of the cell. It

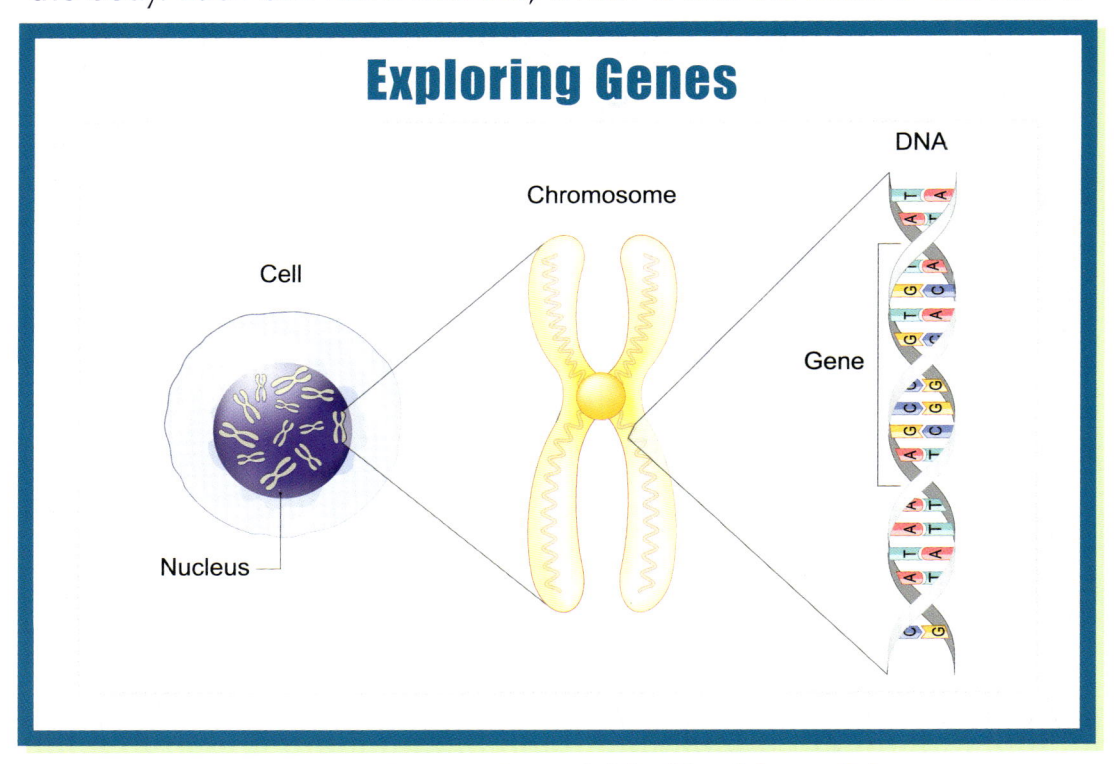

Exploring Genes

DNA

Chromosome

Cell

Gene

Nucleus

This diagram shows how cells contain nuclei. Inside of the nuclei are chromosomes, which contain genes that are segments of DNA.

directs the cell's actions and determines the organism's features. That's because the nucleus holds chromosomes. These threadlike structures are made up of DNA, which is like the organism's blueprint.

DNA is packed super tightly into a chromosome. In fact, though chromosomes are too small to see without microscopes, all the DNA packed into one chromosome is about 6 feet (2 meters) long stretched end to end. DNA's ladder shape holds rungs made up of pairs of chemicals that tell the body to do certain things.

How does DNA instruct the body? Segments of DNA are called genes, which add up to an organism's genetic code. Most humans have 23 pairs of chromosomes in their cells, which hold about 20,000 genes. The genes instruct the body to make certain proteins. Proteins do much of the work in a body. They decide an organism's traits. When an organism reproduces, it passes on its genes to the next generation.

All humans have about 99.6 percent of their genes in common. Identical twins share even more genetic material. That's why they often look the same.

Siblings often have similar but not the same traits. Their genes came from the same place, but their "code" is a little different.

THE SCIENCE OF REPRODUCTION

When one or two organisms produce offspring, it's called reproduction. In asexual reproduction, one parent organism makes a copy of itself. The offspring is an exact copy. This can happen in some species of plants and animals, especially when there are no mates available.

In sexual reproduction, two organisms come together to produce offspring. The offspring has half of one parent's genes and half of the other parent's genes. The genes are present in egg and sperm cells, and the combination of genes creates a new genetic code. Reproduction is how genes are passed to a new generation of organisms.

Fast Fact

Sperm and egg cells are the sex cells that are used for reproduction. Biologically male people usually have sperm cells, while biologically female people usually have egg cells.

The Perfect Pair

In most human cells, you'll find 46 chromosomes. However, in sperm and egg cells, there's one set of 23 chromosomes. They join with the other to make a full set of 46 chromosomes. That's why you might have your dad's nose but your mom's eye color. You get a little bit from both.

What happens after the egg and sperm unite? The cell that's created starts to divide over and over again. It becomes an **embryo**, and then eventually grows into a baby with the new genetic code stitched into every one of its cells. Each gene determines the baby's traits, from curly hair to freckles.

All About Alleles

In a chromosomal pair, there are two versions of each gene. Each parent gives one of these versions. The different versions are called alleles. The person may be born with two different alleles or two of the same alleles. Dominant alleles are those that are "stronger," or more likely to show up as traits. For example, the gene for brown hair is strong, so a person with a brown-haired parent is likely to get that dominant trait.

Recessive alleles show up as traits only if a person gets two copies of the same gene. For example, red hair is recessive. If one parent has the gene for red hair, but the other does not, their child will not have red hair.

Red is the rarest hair color in the world, occurring in only about 2 percent of the world's population.

NATURE VS. NURTURE

People often wonder if a person's physical features and behavior are impacted by nature (genes) or nurture (the environment in which they're raised). It's a little bit of both! Genes affect a person's natural hair, eye, and skin colors, for example. They may impact body type as well, but what a person eats and how they move their body also has a big impact on how their body looks and works.

Imagine that a person is great at basketball. Their father was also great at basketball, so people say it must be genetic. However, that person was probably around basketball a lot in their life because of their father. It's hard to tell if nature or nurture made the person good at basketball, but likely it was a combination of many things.

Nature may affect your height and strength, which can make certain sports easier for you, but growing up in a sports-focused environment can do that too!

A person would need the red hair gene on both sides of their family to have red hair themselves.

Male or Female?

Chromosomes determine if a person is born with either male or female sex **characteristics**. Someone with female sex characteristics receives an X chromosome from their mother and an X chromosome from their father. Someone with male sex characteristics receives

Identical twins are the same sex. Fraternal twins, or those with different genes, can be the same or different.

Sex Determination in Humans

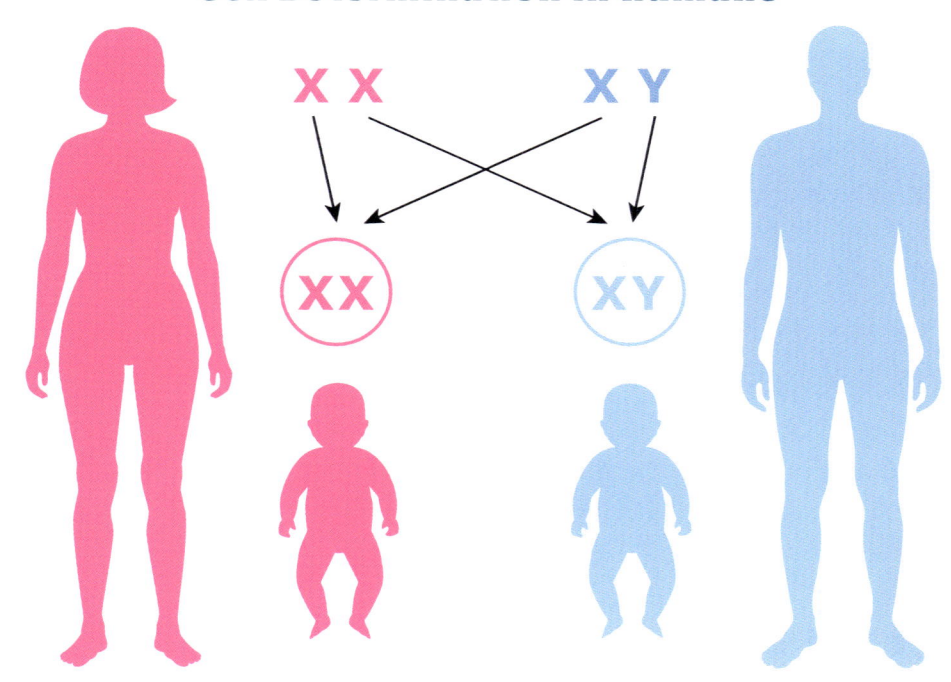

The sex of a baby is determined at fertilization. This diagram shows the different ways X and Y chromosomes can be inherited from parents.

an X chromosome from their mother and a Y chromosome from their father. This happens at fertilization, or the moment the egg and sperm cells come together.

Sex chromosomes impact a human's sexual organs and some physical characteristics. However, they don't necessarily determine a person's **gender**.

The genotype and phenotype for feather color is different in some flamingos based on what they eat.

INHERITED TRAITS

If you studied a person's DNA, you would be looking at their genotype. An organism's genotype is what's written in their genetic code. However, if you were just to look at the person, you would see their phenotype.

Phenotype is how a genotype presents physically in an organism. This includes observable traits such as skin color and height. While the genotype is directly linked to the genes present in a person, the phenotype can also be affected by the environment. For example, a person may have the gene for light-colored skin, but may live in a place with a lot of sun, causing their skin to tan.

Physical Features

Take a moment to write down your own physical traits. You may note your facial features. Maybe you have brown eyes. Maybe you have dimples in your cheeks. Start to think of what features you may have inherited from your parents.

Some traits are easy to observe. Can you roll your

Fast Fact

Flamingos have genes for white feathers. However, they eat pink shrimp, which makes their feathers turn pink.

tongue into a taco shape? That's one trait that is passed from parents to their offspring, but also something that may be learned over time. Do you have freckles? These are inherited, but are also influenced by the time a person spends in the sun. Are your earlobes "attached" (connected to your head) or "detached" (hanging like a raindrop)? This trait is easy to observe and is not influenced by the environment at all.

Hair texture is mostly controlled by genes. Curly, wavy, or straight hair often runs in families and even across **ethnicities**. However, many genes control this trait, so while it runs in families, it's sometimes hard to predict.

Hereditary Health

You may think everyone has the same risk for getting diseases or that only environmental factors cause illness. However, genetics plays a role in the health conditions that people develop. For example, you are more at risk for heart disease and high blood pressure if these run in your family. Having asthma or diabetes in your family also increases your risk for developing these issues. People with a history of hereditary health issues can decrease their risks by eating foods with a variety of nutrients, moving their body, and avoiding harmful substances.

Certain **cancers** also run in families. Scientists found gene mutations that can cause breast cancer. This has led to more people getting screened for cancer and taking steps to stay healthy.

People with asthma might carry an inhaler, which is a tool to help them breathe if they have an asthma attack.

Fast Fact

Asthma causes attacks of breathlessness, coughing, and wheezing. Triggers include smoke and mold. People with a personal or family history of asthma can try to avoid these triggers.

GENETIC DISORDERS

Sometimes an organism's genetic code is different from average. That can cause health problems. Genetic disorders can be inherited from parents. They can also be caused by a change in a gene on the chromosome, called a mutation; a missing part of a chromosome, called a deletion; or genes shifting to the wrong chromosome, called a translocation. Sometimes there's an extra chromosome or a missing chromosome.

One genetic disorder is Down syndrome. It's caused by an extra copy of chromosome 21. People with Down syndrome often have characteristic facial features and some degree of intellectual disability. About 1 in every 755 babies born in the United States has this genetic disorder.

Down syndrome is the most common chromosome condition in the United States.

Abilities and Behaviors

Have you ever been told that you inherited your math skills from your mother or your musical abilities from your father? Maybe people say that art or athletic abilities "run in the family." Studies have found that there is some genetic link for musical creativity, intelligence, and athletic ability. However, hours of practice, nutrition, and educational opportunities also make a big difference.

Behaviors can also be impacted by genetics. For example, studies have found a genetic link in people's sleep schedules and sleep needs. There are also genetic links in people's personalities and mental illnesses.

Fast Fact

Genetic studies are often done on identical twins because they share so much of their DNA. This can let scientists know if their abilities or behaviors are a result of genetics, environment, or both.

You may have inherited music ability, but practice time and opportunities make a large difference in talent as well.

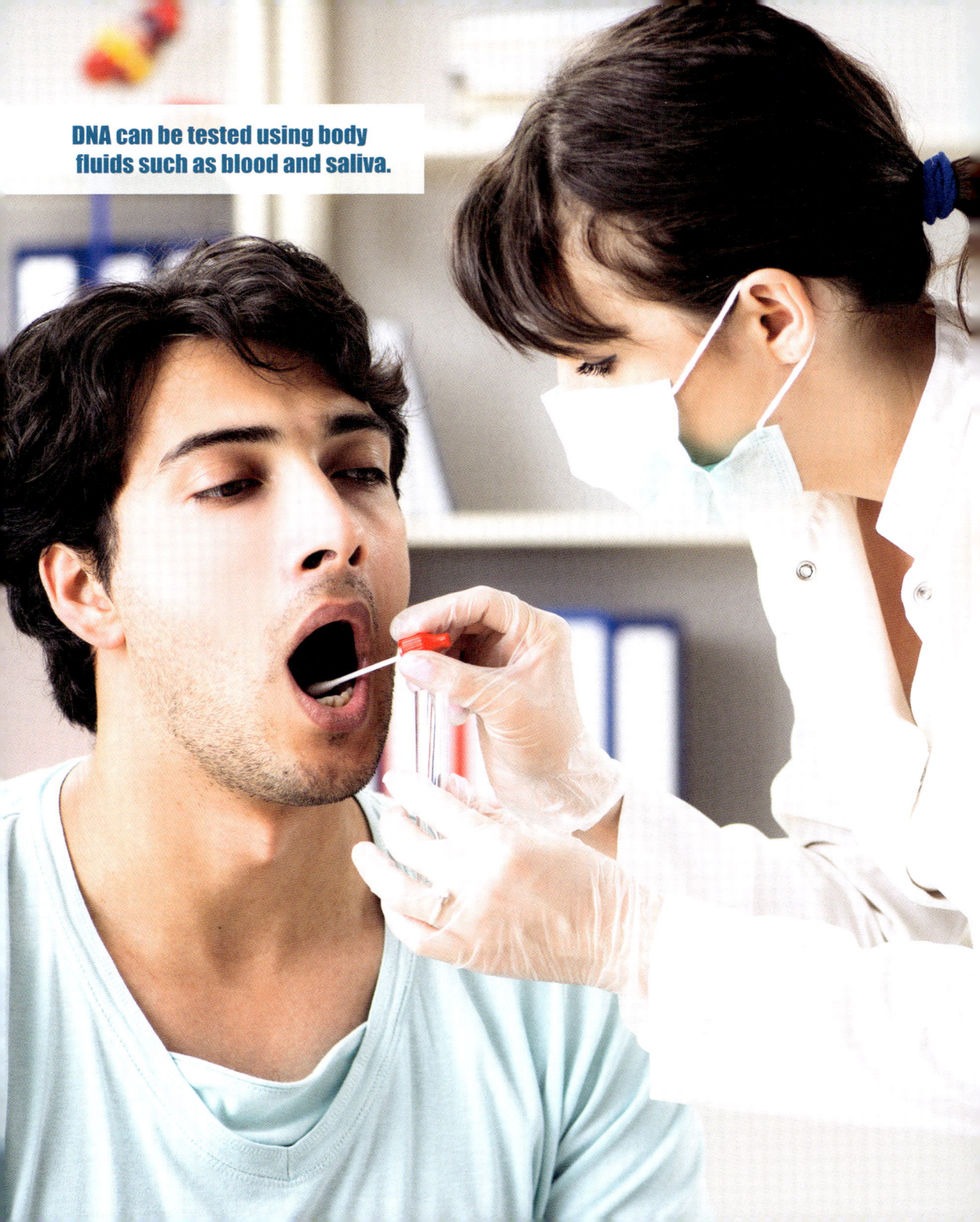
DNA can be tested using body fluids such as blood and saliva.

HOW CAN WE USE GENETICS?

Genes affect how a person looks, how they act, and what talents they have. They affect their current health and the possibilities for health problems in the future. For better or worse, genes have a large impact on the lives of humans and all other living things.

Scientists have studied genes for many years. In 1990, scientists with the Human **Genome** Project started creating a **sequence** of the human genome. The project was finished in 2003, providing invaluable research to help advance medicine and the study of genetics. People are now using DNA research to learn more about themselves. How can genetics be used to help the human race?

Genetic Engineering

Scientists have used their knowledge of genetics to create new treatments, medicines, and plants. Genetic engineering is **modifying** DNA to change an organism or a population of organisms. In many cases, new genes are placed into a strain of bacteria that copies over

Fast Fact

Some companies use DNA to tell people about their family history and health risks.

and over within the organism. One success of genetic engineering was the production of human insulin, which regulates blood sugar. This product saves the lives of people with diabetes.

Genetically engineered plants have also been developed. Plants can be engineered to avoid diseases, thrive in certain conditions, and kill pests. This means more crops to eat and use.

Most corn in the United States is a GMO. It was developed to keep pests away.

Cloning

You may look a lot like your parent, but you're not an exact copy of them. However, scientists have developed the ability to clone certain organisms. Cloning is creating an exact copy of a cell or whole organism. This is normal for simple organisms such as bacteria, but not for complex organisms such as plants, animals, and people.

The first animal cloning success was Dolly the Sheep, born in 1996 in Scotland. It took 227 tries! Cloned embryos often die before developing into a baby. After Dolly was born, scientists also successfully cloned mice, dogs, and pigs.

Dolly the Sheep lived about seven years, dying in 2003.

Are humans next? Right now, cloning humans goes against many laws and an international declaration from the United Nations.

Gene Therapy

In genetic engineering, an organism's DNA is modified, or changed, to **enhance** its abilities or features. In gene therapy, an organism's DNA is modified to prevent or treat genetic diseases. This can be helpful for people with diseases such as **cystic fibrosis** or the blood disorder hemophilia. It can also help people with certain cancers.

The most common way to introduce healthy genes into the body is through viruses. The virus would have genes to stop disease in it. When introduced into a person's body, these genes would replace the genes that cause disease. Most gene therapy patients today are part of clinical trials, or a development step before it becomes a widely used treatment.

ETHICAL ISSUES

From the beginning of genetic engineering, cloning, and gene therapy, there have been arguments around if these practices are ethical, or morally "right." Some people think it's okay to clone animals, but not humans. Others think cloning in general is wrong. Some people worry what might happen to the next generation after genetic experiments. When it comes to genetic engineering, some worry that people will start using it to create humans with super abilities and "ideal" features. They worry that people would start to make "designer babies," choosing their features instead of letting nature do the work. Gene therapy, because it is meant to treat disease and not enhance a human, is often seen as less problematic.

Someday, gene therapy may be a common treatment for cancer.

1. Which of your traits resemble your parents'?

2. Which do you think is more important in determining who a person is: nature or nurture?

3. Do you have any abilities or behaviors that "run in the family"?

4. What are some concerns people may have about cloning humans?

GLOSSARY

ancestor: One of the organisms from whom another is descended.

breed: To produce new plants or animals.

cancer: A disease caused by the uncontrolled growth of cells in the body.

characteristic: A distinguishing trait, quality, or property.

cystic fibrosis: A genetic condition that affects the respiratory and digestive systems.

embryo: An animal in the early stages of growth.

enhance: To improve something.

ethnicity: The shared national or cultural identity of a group of people.

gender: The state of being male, female, some combination of the two, or neither male nor female.

generation: A group of living things born and living during the same time.

genome: The complete set of genes present in a cell or organism.

modify: To change something.

monk: A member of a religious order who lives in a monastery.

sequence: A continuous or connected series.

FIND OUT MORE

Books

Claybourne, Anna. *The Science of Me*. London, UK: Wayland Publishing, 2023.

Croy, Anita. *Charles Darwin*. St. Catherine's, ON: Crabtree Publishing Company, 2023.

O'Daly, Anne. *The Basics of Genetics*. New York, NY: The Rosen Publishing Group, 2023.

Websites

Mendel and Inheritance
www.ducksters.com/science/biology/mendel_and_inheritance.php
Find out more about Gregor Mendel's work on inheritance.

What Is a Gene?
kidshealth.org/en/kids/what-is-gene.html
Learn more about genes with this interesting resource from KidsHealth.

What's It Like to Have Down Syndrome?
kids.nationalgeographic.com/pages/article/down-syndrome
Read this first-person account from a girl with a chromosomal difference—Down syndrome.

INDEX